Original title:
The Attic of Forgotten Words

Copyright © 2025 Creative Arts Management OÜ
All rights reserved.

Author: Wyatt Kensington
ISBN HARDBACK: 978-1-80587-207-8
ISBN PAPERBACK: 978-1-80587-677-9

Haunting Melodies of Memory

In a dusty room, the echoes play,
Old tunes jive in a quirky way.
That sock I lost still waltzes near,
With past mistakes, it does a cheer.

The ghost of lunch I couldn't eat,
Spins around on quicksilver feet.
Laughing at the shoes I chose,
As if my taste was ever posed.

A spider's web sings ancient rhymes,
Holding whispers of forgotten crimes.
Chasing shadows that just won't stay,
While I dance in my own ballet.

The clock ticks loud, it's out of tune,
Barking dogs join a fading croon.
Memories drip like melting cheese,
The nonsense of life, a silly tease.

An Archive of Unsaid Words

Piled high on shelves, they gather dust,
Lost thoughts in a bubble of rust.
For every secret I did not say,
A funny face comes out to play.

Words tickle me, like peeking cats,
Whispering tales about old hats.
A jargon of giggles, puns galore,
Where silence meets the funny score.

Conversations trapped in pickle jars,
Each phrase inside has battle scars.
With rhymes that roll like doughy balls,
And punchlines hiding in four walls.

In this vault of quirky thinks,
I find solace in silly links.
Merriment floats like fluff on cream,
A comedy sketch, a waking dream.

Reflections in a Forgotten Mirror

Cracks reveal the laughter I hid,
Reflecting moments that life did bid.
Each shard a tale of trips and spins,
Of quirky losses and silly wins.

The glass giggles as I lean close,
With secrets that the room's the most.
An image jumps, a mocking grin,
Of yesterday's woes, tossed in a bin.

Fuzzy eyebrows, hair askew,
Dancing to jokes from a tarnished view.
My past winks as I strike a pose,
In a mirror where humor grows.

Time's a trickster, sly and sweet,
Turning woes into silly beats.
So here I stand, all patched and bright,
In giggly warmth, what a delight!

Tales Beneath the Roof

Up above, a broom does dance,
With dust bunnies that take a chance.
They play poker, they hold their cards,
While old shoes cheer, saying 'Aloha'!

A sock lost its match in a feud,
It felt lonely, but stayed quite crude.
A hat speaks loudly about its glory,
To a stepladder, it tells its story.

Untold Stories in the Dark

In shadows deep, the spiders spin,
Webs of laughter where dreams begin.
A sandwich whispers, 'I'm still fresh!'
To a pickle who claims, 'I'm the best!'

A rubber band stretches tales so wide,
Of slingshot fits and leaps of pride.
They giggle and roll, no one can hear,
The secrets shared, away from fear.

Fables of Forgotten Feelings

Old teapots gossip, brewing cheer,
While kettle drums keep spirits near.
A mug with a chip cracks jokes all day,
'Til spilled tea blabs, 'You're full of fray!'

A rubber ducky rolls its eyes,
As a mop sings out in heartfelt sighs.
They ponder plans of a woeful fate,
Yet laugh it off, they're never late.

Remnants of a Silent Vocabulary

Words piled high like forgotten toys,
Under the floor, they make some noise.
'Hey, remember when we were all cool?'
Said the verb to a rather shy jewel.

An adverb winks, quite sly and bold,
To a noun that claims it's 'twice as old.'
They chuckle and weave a tangled rhyme,
In the quiet chaos, they spend their time.

Silenced Sonatas from Above

Upstairs, the symphonies sleep,
Creaking floors where secrets creep.
A trumpet lost, so out of tune,
While violins hum to the moon.

Dust bunnies dance in quiet halls,
Chasing echoes of old calls.
A cello grins, its strings unwound,
In laughter's arms, the notes are found.

An old kazoo, with faded might,
Holds court with shadows in the night.
The piano sighs, its keys look grand,
Yet all it plays is lost on hand.

So raise a glass to tunes long gone,
To melodies that still live on.
Though silence reigns, it's not the end,
For in our hearts, the music bends.

Cobwebbed Compositions

In corners thick with spider threads,
Lie songs unclaimed, and words like beds.
A waltz once danced on breezy days,
Now tangled up in time's bizarre ways.

An opera's whisper, soft yet bold,
Is caught within the dust, so old.
While rhythm takes a nap, quite deep,
As laughter's shadow starts to creep.

With puns and jokes that time forgot,
In boxes stacked, they tie the knot.
So listen close, to laughs concealed,
In cobwebbed silence, joy revealed.

The melodies, though twisted tight,
Still dream of one more glorious night.
For in the hush, there's room to play,
And humor lives in every sway.

The Vault of Silent Voices

Inside a chest, the voices dwell,
Each one a tale too strange to tell.
A chorus of quirks, bizarre yet shy,
Echoes of laughter that flutter by.

They sing of socks, mismatched and wild,
Of kitchen mishaps, and garlic mild.
A trumpet's fart, a clarinet's sneeze,
Funny old tales that bring us ease.

Whispers bounce off the wooden beams,
Like wayward children with goofy dreams.
An accordion hides behind a shoe,
Playing a tune that's far from true.

Though silence shrouds the dusty space,
There's laughter waiting to embrace.
For in the vault, where humor thrives,
The echo of joy forever lives.

Fragments from the Heights

On rickety shelves, the fragments lay,
Comedic scripts from yesterday.
With missing pages, they still convene,
In a riotous plot, yet unseen.

A joke book singing from its spine,
About a fish that drank some wine.
A parody of socks on heads,
While snoring echoes from the beds.

The jokes may flop, yet still they shine,
Each punchline tangled in design.
These fragments jive in wild delight,
Turning silence into pure insight.

So gather round for tales untold,
Of socked-footed ninjas, brave and bold.
For in the heights, where whispers swirl,
Laughter waits to give a twirl.

The Crypt of Lost Expressions

In the crypt where giggles hide,
Lurks a pun that fell aside.
A joke left hanging on a nail,
Wishing for a laugh to sail.

Whispers of a snickered tale,
Echo where the old words fail.
A rhyme with a comical twist,
Seems too funny to resist!

Forgotten lines, they dance about,
In this space, there's no doubt.
They trip over their own wit,
Until their punchlines finally split.

So come and find that silly jest,
Hidden here, it takes a rest.
In the crypt where words decay,
Laughter rolls the dust away!

Buried Words Beneath Beams

Beneath the beams, a rhyme sleeps tight,
Hiding from the morning light.
Whimsical phrases, buried deep,
Awaiting a chuckle, a giggle to keep.

A quip from long forgotten days,
Wanders through this dusty maze.
A slip of tongue, a missed remark,
Ready to ignite that spark.

Puns and jests, wrapped in cloth,
Wait for someone to take an oath.
To unearth the joy tucked away,
With each laugh, they start to play.

So lift that beam, dig in with glee,
Find that silly word, oh me!
Beneath the beams, they long to rise,
With a laugh and a grin, to claim the skies!

Lingering Phrases in Attic Air

In attic air, the echoes cling,
To slippery words that dance and swing.
A banter once clever, now just a tease,
Waiting for chuckles, if you please.

Phrases that flutter like wayward bees,
Buzzing softly with whimsical ease.
They whisper secrets on dust-laden shelves,
Hints of humor, they jest themselves.

A goofy mix of sentences free,
Hoping someone will find the glee.
Like socks that wander, lost on purpose,
Curious jabs waiting, oh that's the surface!

So breathe in deep that funny air,
Words that linger, beyond a glare.
In this space, let's have some fun,
As laughter dances, it's just begun!

Abandoned Lines of Lore

In corners dim, where dust bunnies lay,
Abandoned lines wish for a play.
A story forgotten, a tale gone stale,
Yet humor remains, like a whimsical trail.

Jokes left on hangers, their punchlines worn,
Waiting for laughter, forlorn and torn.
They wiggle their words in playful plight,
Calling for someone to ignite the light.

A riddle that rolls with a ticklish tease,
Sits in the corner, just waiting to please.
But time has postponed this giggly affair,
Until someone dares to share in the air.

So sweep away dust, clear the way,
For abandoned lines yearning to play.
In a forgotten nook, they beckon and twirl,
Let's take them out for a jesting whirl!

Forgotten Tomes and Tattered Dreams

Books piled high with tales so light,
Each one whispers, 'Read me tonight!'
Dust bunnies dance on the shelves above,
Wondering if they'll ever find love.

Old pages chuckle, some are quite bold,
Sharing secrets we never were told.
A romance scene making us shriek,
While reciting great haikus, quite unique!

Lost are the stories of dragon and knight,
Replaced by cat memes, oh what a sight!
Beneath these tomes, a sandwich lies,
Wondering why it receives no cries.

With cobwebs thick, and giggles too,
These forgotten tales still feel brand new.
Each turn of phrase a funny dance,
Come join the fun, take a chance!

Threads of Silence Woven Tight

In corners dark, where shadows creep,
Lie tales that giggle, secrets that peep.
A spider's web, so grand and neat,
Holds a joke with a punchline sweet.

Whispers linger, in silence they twine,
Bantering softly in a quiet line.
A sock from laundry plays the fool,
While books in repose look ever so cool.

With every thread, a laughter soars,
Echoes of clumsiness fill up the floors.
Cobbled thoughts knit in absurd hats,
Spitting stories like tongue-tied chats.

This fabric of silence, oddly bright,
Crafts a tapestry full of delight.
From whispers to chuckles, woven just right,
Even silence knows how to ignite!

Fragments of What Once Was

Scattered shards of forgotten fun,
Where once there danced a wild run.
A rubber chicken makes a bold remark,
While old shoes play in the park.

Jumbled thoughts in a jar of clay,
Each holds a laugh for a rainy day.
A paper hat, once grand and square,
Now 'king' of the clutter without a care.

An old joke-book with riddles galore,
Answers lost, but laughter's in store.
A memory of pie fights and cream,
Floating still in a dreamer's gleam.

Though fragments fade and tales may stall,
Hilarity lingers, the best of all.
In a world of pieces, here we rejoice,
For in every scrap, we still have a voice!

The Weight of Dusty Memories

Memories stacked like old newsprint,
Each one a giggle, a cheeky hint.
Dust motes twirl in the sunlight's beam,
Revealing tales like a wild daydream.

A jester's cap from a forgotten play,
Whispers of laughter won't fade away.
They remind us of moments, silly and bright,
Where joy peeked out in the dead of night.

The weight of dust, a playful load,
Each speck a hint, a chuckling code.
Old postcards from friends we forgot,
Bring back grins from the stories they've got.

So lift the lid, don't hesitate,
These dusty gems sure cultivate.
In the weight of memories, wonders unfold,
A carnival of laughter, pure gold!

Unwritten Letters in Trapped Air

In sealed envelopes, jokes lay tight,
They giggle softly, out of sight.
Postage due on winks and sighs,
Check the stamps, and hear their cries.

A paper plane with a folded grin,
Dares to soar, but can't begin.
Whispers stuck, like gum in hair,
Waiting for someone to declare.

Oh, the wishes penned in haste,
Dreams turned stale, too much to taste.
The parchment laughs, with ink made bold,
Stories untold, forever cold.

So here we sit, with pens in hand,
While giggles linger, unplanned and grand.
Let's tease the echoes in the air,
Unwritten love notes, a snare beyond compare.

The Dusty Corners of Memory

In corners where lost socks reside,
Eras of laughter choose to hide.
Faded tales with cobweb threads,
Tickle our brains, like old bread spreads.

Mismatched shoes tell stories bold,
Of dances missed and secrets told.
Dust bunnies scheme in playful rows,
Guiding lost thoughts as nobody knows.

Old photographs with goofy grins,
Capture moments, where no one wins.
Yet they shimmer with joy and cheer,
Reminding aches, to disappear.

So let's sweep through the veils of time,
Find the punchlines in each rhyme.
Raise a toast to the quirks we've kept,
For in neatness, the fun has wept.

Conversations with Shadows

Shadows gather in a sly parade,
Trading secrets in playful shade.
They whisper jokes, with a flicker and spin,
While I pretend I'm not listening in.

Bump into laughter that glides and slips,
As moonlight dances on their cryptic quips.
'Did you hear how that light bulb died?'
The shadows chuckle, a carefree ride.

I offer a pun on the way they stretch,
But all they do is giggle and sketch.
In the dim light, they weave their tales,
Painting the night with invisible trails.

So join this chat, in the twilight glow,
With shades of laughter that ebb and flow.
In the corners where echoes meet,
Find humor hiding beneath your feet.

Requiem for Lost Phrases

Oh, the phrases that take a snooze,
Caught in a dream of forgetful blues.
"Where did you go?" they wail and sigh,
As metaphors flutter, kiss the sky.

Once bold declarations turned to mist,
Resurrect them with a scoff and twist.
Limericks hiding in the dust,
Awaiting a chance to regain their lust.

But laughter's the key, to bring them back,
With knock-knock jokes, and a hearty snack.
Let's host a funeral for all that's lost,
Where funny is free, no matter the cost.

So raise a glass to words that roam,
With laughter in heart, they find their home.
A requiem sung, in goofy glee,
For every phrase that used to be.

Forgotten Lullabies

In a corner, whispers sleep,
Teddy bears in piles, oh so steep.
Socks without partners, they're on a strike,
Crooning softly, just like a bike.

Dust bunnies dance, a waltz so grand,
As other toys take a stand.
A playful tune floats on the air,
Melodies tangled in a teddy bear's hair.

Pajamas hang like ghosts of the past,
Dreams remembered, but fading fast.
Rabbits giggle, tucked in tight,
'What a riot!' they squeal in delight.

Blankets crumpled, a cozy throne,
Count the stars, then snore like a drone.
Lullabies chuckle, lost in the haze,
Sailing on whims, 'neath the moon's gaze.

Requiem for Abandoned Dreams

Once a plane made of cardboard flew,
Now it's a hat for the cat named Blue.
Unfinished stories, half-hearted schemes,
Rest on the shelf in muffled screams.

A racecar lost its thrilling speed,
Now it's a chair for a dust mite's need.
Heroic quests in a shoebox grave,
With action figures that lost their brave.

Forgotten wishes covered in dust,
Left behind, left to rust.
Riddles left unsolved, oh what a waste,
They giggle together, a hapless haste.

Will-o'-the-wisps dance without care,
While shoes live on with stories to share.
In this jest lies a bittersweet laughter,
For dreams are silly, ever after.

Songs from the Loft

A ukulele strums a silliness song,
While spatulas dance, where they don't belong.
A dreary old lamp blinks its eye,
To an off-key tune that makes dust fly.

Old records spin tales of delight,
About a cat that twirled all night.
Pillows snicker at rhythms unplanned,
As shoes join in, forming a band.

Out of tune, in a melodious clatter,
Echoes of laughter grow louder, what's the matter?
With each silly note, they frolic and sway,
In the loft where lost things come out to play.

Clocks tick-tock in a hastened dance,
Giving the junk a humorous chance.
A symphony of nonsense brightens the gloom,
In a concert hall made of objects in bloom.

Relics of Rhyme

Once upon a whimsically day,
Words shuffled 'round, in playful sway.
Fairy tales hiding beneath old chairs,
Laughing at life without any cares.

The spoons sing, clinging to pots,
While slippers giggle, tying their knots.
Old rhymes scurry, too proud to collect,
With verses of nonsense that we all neglect.

A glove tells tales of a long-lost friend,
While mirrors chuckle at tales they amend.
In forgotten lines, they shimmy and jive,
Breaking the silence, so glad to be alive.

Where letters linger, and laughter prevails,
In a dusty reset of whimsical tales.
Relics of rhyme dance in the glow,
Spinning their stories from long ago.

Reveries in Dust-Caked Pages

In corners dark, a tale does slide,
Where ancient thoughts and jokes collide.
A rumble here, a giggle there,
Words once lively, now full of air.

Forgotten puns on crinkled sheets,
Declare their fate in whispered beats.
A quip from times both odd and grand,
Tickles the mind like an unseen hand.

There's humor trapped in bygone lore,
Like socks that vanish, who keeps score?
Dust balls dance, while pages grin,
As laughter echoes softly in.

From cracked spines rise a cheeky cheer,
Awake the tales we're glad to hear.
Each laugh revived, a spark just bright,
In dust and dreams, we find delight.

Ethereal Echoes in Twilight

The ink runs dry, yet jokes still flow,
Under the watch of moonlit glow.
Lost whispers hum of silly fights,
Confessions made on dim, funny nights.

A ghostly jest from ages past,
With every chuckle, shadows cast.
In this twilight, glee holds sway,
As echoes dance and drift away.

Mismatched rhymes and playful tones,
Steal the show like quirky clones.
Each fading word a clumsy fall,
Yet in that stumble, we hear it all.

Twilight grins, where silence bends,
And laughter's warmth till daylight ends.
A merry haunt for hearts once shy,
Where ethereal giggles never die.

Faded Whispers of Nostalgia

In closets tight, old tales entwine,
With laughter lines, and pop's decline.
A postcard joke from years ago,
Still shines despite its yellowed glow.

Friends who penned with clumsy hands,
Leave quirky lists of ghostly plans.
Remember when that word was cool?
Now it's a relic, a silly tool.

Nostalgia dances on worn-out chairs,
Where echoes live and no one dares.
A chuckle here, a grin pulled tight,
As faded whispers spark delight.

In every cranny, laughter hides,
With snickers waiting, it abides.
We sift through life with twinkling eyes,
To find the joy where memory lies.

The Sepulcher of Speech

In burial grounds of weary wit,
The words lay still, a jumbled fit.
A joker's tomb, where laughter sleeps,
With silly quips, the silence seeps.

Old jokes laid down like dusty bones,
Awaiting friends with phone-honed tones.
To raise a laugh or wake a pun,
From sepulchers of speech undone.

In hushed tones, we fear the night,
While memes of old begin to bite.
Each ghostly grin that haunts the eaves,
Brings back the joy that never leaves.

So let us gather in this plot,
Where echoes ring and laughs are caught.
For every word that fades away,
Can rise again and play all day.

The Lexicon of Loneliness

In the corner, a dusty tome,
With words that never found a home.
They giggle and chuckle, waiting still,
For someone to spill a funny quill.

An adjective's lost its sense of flair,
While verbs in pajamas dance in despair.
Conjunctions whisper jokes with pride,
But only the mice are qualified.

Each page holds tales of awkward dates,
Where nouns got tangled in tangled plates.
Adverbs fell over, clutching their sides,
As laughter echoed through the slide.

So here's to words that never got said,
To lonely terms that dream instead.
If only laughter could be released,
The lexicon would be quite the feast!

Unwritten Prose Under the Eaves

Beneath the eaves, there's a blank sheet,
With scribbles of nonsense, oh so sweet.
The lines of comedy long to play,
But dust settles funny in disarray.

An adverb sneezes, causing a ruckus,
While nouns quip and sing without fuss.
"Let's write a tale," the verbs implore,
But the pen rolls away, forever more.

The metaphors hide, playing peek-a-boo,
As hyperboles boast and shout, "Look at you!"
Unwritten prose in a playful fight,
With laughter trapped until the night.

So let's throw confetti on ink so rare,
And dance with the whispers that fill the air.
Let's make a story that tickles our hearts,
With words that bring joy as their funny parts!

Echoing Penumbra

In the shadowy corners where echoes creep,
Lies a chorus of words that can't help but leap.
"Tell us a joke!" the syllables call,
As the questions tumble and giggles enthrall.

Puns in the twilight begin to collide,
While past participles roll off with pride.
They trip over commas and waddle away,
Creating a ruckus, a grand cabaret.

Each echo a fragment of laughter long due,
A whimsical wordplay, so utterly new.
They twirl through the dark, seeking a friend,
And the giggling phrases can never quite end.

So dance with the shadows, let nonsense unfurl,
In the penumbra where funny dreams swirl.
With echoes of laughter within every space,
We find joy in the words that leave a trace!

Sentiments in Solitary Silence

In stillness, where forgotten thoughts rest,
There's a solitude wrapped in humor's jest.
Sentiments giggle, whispering low,
As they ponder the puns only they know.

Each lonely phrase wears a quirky disguise,
With punchlines hidden from curious eyes.
"Hey, what's the deal?" a question does peep,
But dreams of laughter lie still in their sleep.

They balance their gags on a velvet thread,
With ifs and buts stuck on words left unsaid.
An exclamation point jumps in surprise,
As solitude snickers, rolling its eyes.

So let's lift the silence and give it a whirl,
With sentiments ready to twist and twirl.
For even in silence, smiles can ignite,
In the company of phrases seeking the light!

A Symphony of Silent Echoes

In the corner, a shoe with a life,
Tells tales of a cat and a knife.
Who'd have thought it could sing so loud?
How did it get lost in this crowd?

A hat with a frown and a feather,
Wishes for wind, but it's tethered.
It dreams of a stroll in the park,
Instead, it just gathers up dark.

A clock that forgot how to tick,
Once counted each moment with a click.
Now it just hangs, looking quite bored,
Waiting for joy to stop and accord.

In this place of lost and the weird,
Oddities smile, maybe they're cheered.
Laughter erupts from dusty old chairs,
As echoes of fun float up the stairs.

Timeworn Stories Awaiting

A fish on a shelf in a dusty jar,
Claims it once danced with a Neptunian star.
The seaweed's still stuck in its teeth,
Oh, what a catch, yet it knows no relief!

Old boots hold secrets of muddy delight,
They trod through the past in a wild, crazy night.
With each step, they'd clink and they'd clatter,
Ushering laughter, not a hint of a batter.

An umbrella, too proud, with rust on its ribs,
Mourns for the rain that departed in dribs.
Now it just guards a gathering of traps,
Wishing for showers and spontaneous naps.

In shadows reside quirky reflections,
Life in odd shapes, like wild collections.
Stories await in each quirky nook,
An eccentric tale in every old book.

Fleeting Whispers of the Past

A spoon with a grin and a chip on its side,
Danced with a fork, but the knife was denied.
They twirled 'round the table, a mischievous spree,
In a battle of wits: who cooks best tea?

A dusty old lamp that flickers in glee,
Remembers the parties, oh, how they'd be!
With each twist of the bulb, memories spark,
A light-show of laughter that brightens the dark.

Old records spin with a creaky old sound,
Each scratch tells a story of times that were found.
They hum of adventures, both silly and grand,
As dust bunnies jig to the music unplanned.

In corners accumulate echoes so wise,
A treasure trove full of comical sighs.
Time slips away on this whimsical ride,
Where whispers of joy and nostalgia collide.

Charcoal Lines on Yellowed Pages

A scribble of dreams on a page from the past,
Shows a goat in a tux, dancing real fast.
The ink's a bit smudged, but the joy's still clear,
It's a sight that could make any grump disappear!

Old sketches of cats wearing hats, oh so bright,
Prance with a wiggle in the pale moonlight.
They plot silly capers, it's all quite absurd,
And here in this space, there's no need for a word.

A poem that rhymes about socks that can fly,
Takes flight through the attic, oh my, oh my!
Who knew that a thing so mundane could ignite,
A flurry of laughter that takes flight at night?

With every loose page, a smile springs forth,
A world full of whimsy, of endless worth.
In the corners, creations make hearts dance,
Where joy is preserved and memories prance.

Whispered Wishes in Dust

In corners where odd notions dwell,
A sock debates a broken bell.
They whisper secrets, nothing grand,
Like how to dance, or how to stand.

A hat confesses, it feels so lost,
Dancing with dust at quite the cost.
The broom sibling hums a spry tune,
While the old toy waits for a full moon.

A coat of moths spins tales at dusk,
Of bread that dreamed, but turned to husk.
They giggle softly at all things missed,
Like runaway shoes in a plumed twist.

So join the party of things unseen,
Where dust bunnies reign in a velvet sheen.
Each whispered wish in the musty haze,
Finds joy in the silly, in all odd ways.

Echo Chamber of Lost Words

In this chamber where echoes play,
A 'whoops' and a 'wow' scampers away.
Converse with nothing, have a big laugh,
As 'oops' tries to tell a selfie's half.

A clangy pot sings, 'I've lost my lid!'
While spatulas train for a kitchen bid.
They're practicing lines for a flair parade,
Hoping this time, they won't be delayed.

An old pen named Rusty can hardly write,
Proclaims it's too tired for another fight.
Yet still scribbles dreams with inkless flair,
Dancing with letters that float in the air.

So in this grand hall of forgotten chatter,
Puns tumble around, and nonsense does flatter.
Join the ruckus, let laughter abound,
In the echo of words yet to be found.

Chronicles of the Overlooked

Behold the tales of a paper clip,
Who fancied itself a mighty ship.
It sailed through sheets and clouds of dust,
Claiming treasures of endless rust.

A jigsaw puzzle with pieces missing,
Hopes to find mates while lightly pissing.
It pops confetti with a satisfying sound,
As each piece shuffles, fun to be found.

The lonely sock sings a ballad of socks,
Who left their mates, like running clocks.
Each verse it croons makes laundry weep,
For mismatched dreams they hope to keep.

Chronicles written in whimsical glee,
Of objects that giggle in silent spree.
With each turn of their fate, they'll rehearse,
The funny sides of the universe.

The Dusty Lexicon

In layers thick, the words bob and weave,
A squabble of verbs like they've something to achieve.
Adjectives dance in their sage attire,
As a noun tells a tale of fiery desire.

The commas gossip, rolling in jest,
While exclamation points throw a wild fest.
Conjunctions trip over their own smooth links,
And the syntax snickers, dodging all blinks.

Old idioms chuckle, their wisdom so sly,
Especially when metaphors soar up high.
They tickle the thoughts in a playful rhyme,
Turning banter into a joyful mime.

So sift through the dust where the pages might flap,
Finding giggles and grins in this easy trap.
In the lexicon gray, let laughter ignite,
What once was forgotten, now dances with light.

Ephemera of Heartfelt Reminiscence

In a box, I found a note,
Written in a cheeky coat,
It said, "Don't eat the yucky pie,"
And now I know just why I cry.

Socks that danced upon the floor,
Once they were, but now no more,
A tale of how they lost their mate,
They're sharp at lying, not at fate.

A clock that laughed, a book that grinned,
Together they would not rescind,
They shared a joke on timeless ways,
Yet tick-tock still misleads our days.

Memories wrapped in silly spray,
They bubble up and float away,
A giggle slipped 'neath dusty beams,
Oh, how they weave the wildest dreams.

A Collection of Faded Whispers

A recipe for purple stew,
It called for cows and maybe glue,
I tried to cook, but what a mess,
The kitchen swam in sheer distress.

A feathered hat, a mismatched shoe,
Once worn by someone wild and true,
They stand in silence, tell no tales,
But in my heart, a laugh prevails.

Old photographs with crooked smiles,
They follow me for countless miles,
Like friends who never seem to leave,
Their joy makes it hard to believe.

A dusty chair that squeaks and sighs,
Just like my dreams of summer skies,
It whispers secrets through the years,
In laughter's echo, melt my fears.

Hidden Harmonies of the Past

A kazoo band from long ago,
They played a tune, yet lo, oh no!
The notes went flying, birds took flight,
They laughed all day, and danced all night.

Tangled strings and mismatched keys,
They played a game with autumn leaves,
Each note a giggle, light and free,
In harmony, they sang to me.

A puzzle piece that doesn't fit,
Yet always finds a way to sit,
Among the laughter, plans so grand,
The mixed-up joy was always planned.

A trumpet kissed by morning dew,
It toots a dream that's strange but true,
In memories wrapped like cotton candy,
The tunes will echo, sweet and dandy.

Shattered Syllables in Shadow

Words like candy, stuck on walls,
They melt away when bedtime calls,
A riddle wrapped in layers thick,
I try to solve, but meet a brick.

Giggling ghosts in borrowed hats,
They prank the night, invite the chats,
In whispers soft, they start to tease,
Their jests a breeze that bends the trees.

A treasure map with crisscross lines,
It leads to pies and rusty pines,
I followed dreams, but found a cat,
Who shared my pie, how 'bout that?

Jumbled phrases, scattered cheer,
They trip and tumble, bring me near,
In this odd jumble, truth's unveiled,
Laughter's where our hearts have sailed.

Lingering in the Dust of Memory

Amidst the junk, old tales reside,
Caught somewhere 'twixt laugh and pride.
A sock with holes, a hat askew,
Whispers of chaos, just a few.

Dust motes dance, pirouetting bright,
A forgotten joke takes off in flight.
The clock, it ticks in comic spans,
While I recount the clumsy plans.

Lurking there, a rubber chicken,
With laughter loud, it stays kickin'.
Beneath the pile, an old bouquet,
That once was fresh, now leads astray.

So here we sit, with quirks to share,
Where every quirk is light as air.
A chorus of ghosts, all in disguise,
Giggling at life through blurry eyes.

The Hushed Chronicle

In the corner waits an ancient tome,
With tales of gnomes who call it home.
Turn the page, a riddle gleams,
Of talking fish and candy streams.

Once a noble knight fell flat,
On a tattered rug, ran off with a cat.
His armor clanked in rhythmic glee,
As if to mock his destiny.

A dusty pen, it tries to write,
But every line is pure delight.
Words tumble out with silly flair,
As if they know they're light as air.

Chasing thoughts like buzzing flies,
In this vault where nonsense lies.
Each yawn becomes a grinning cheer,
As whispers of whimsy float near.

Silenced Syllables of Solitude

In the corner, shadows wait,
With tongues once bold, now locked by fate.
Words flit 'round like butterflies,
Collecting dust with tired sighs.

A rubber plant with tales unknown,
Spouts wisdom in its hushed tone.
But who will listen to the leaves?
They chuckle softly in the eaves.

Forgotten phrases take their rest,
In space where silence creaks its best.
Witty jabs and puns at play,
All vanish in the light of day.

Yet silly echoes find their place,
In this quiet, cozy space.
Where laughter's just a breath away,
And puns emerge to save the day.

The Forgotten Nest of Narratives

Once upon a time, they say,
A sock and shoe had a array.
A battle fought beneath the bed,
With mismatched socks and dreams to spread.

A tiny bird with tales too grand,
Extracted laughs from every strand.
Each yarn recalls a twisty fate,
As laughter lingers, never late.

In shadows deep, a mouse pranced by,
With secret hopes beneath the sky.
His cheese brigade, so proud and bold,
Wrote legends that will never grow old.

So gather round for fun-filled lore,
Of goofy antics and laughs galore.
Where every line's a sweet surprise,
And joy is found in silly sighs.

The Heartbeat of Forgotten Pages

Dust bunnies weave tales of old,
Where scribbles and doodles are bold.
A giggle erupts from a pickle jar,
As memories dance like a friendly tar.

A sock in a corner winks with glee,
Whispers of loves, a curious spree.
Old jokes under boxes, stacked in bizarre,
They chuckle and chortle, oh how bizarre!

Crayons and marbles, a wild parade,
Echoing laughter of moments once made.
Their secret conspire, a whimsical ruse,
In the silence, they gleefully choose.

Words tumble out, like cats in a drawer,
Each with a story, each wanting more.
Funny haikus, they scribble and fade,
In this grand mishmash, no plans are betrayed.

Soliloquy of Lost Voices

Voices all trapped in a jar, oh dear,
Bickering softly, no one can hear.
A toaster sings ballads of burnt toast,
While a rubber duck plans a grand coast.

Comics curl up, tickle their spines,
While marbles debate clever punchlines.
Each echoing laugh, a ghost of the past,
In this gallery, time shuffles fast.

A sock puppet's tale brings giggles and sighs,
As old storybooks plot their next surprise.
With whispers of wisdom and puns all around,
The comical echoes are joyously found.

Peeking from shadows, forgotten and bright,
Old jokes rekindle, giving pure fright.
In this funhouse of whimsy, confusion reigns,
And joy finds a way to break all the chains.

Secrets Beneath the Beams

Under the rafters where dust motes play,
Secrets are giggling, come join the sway.
A can of beans gives wry commentary,
As forgotten cups share their own literary.

Old lovesick notes, so crumpled and sweet,
Whisper of romances that stumbled on feet.
Each creak of the floor, a chuckle or two,
As forgotten confessions embrace the hue.

The spider spins tales, a sticky design,
While moth-eaten dreams sip on moonshine.
What's lost in the beams? A whimsical plight,
Each secret a joke that unfolds in the night.

Old friends of the attic, they gather with glee,
Sharing old stories, just like you and me.
With laughter infectious, they lighten the mood,
In this home for the quirky, joy's included.

Beneath the Layers of Memory

Beneath crumpled papers, a lizard lies flat,
Making a joke about my old hat.
They chuckle in silence, a troupe in disguise,
While moths in the corner share snickers and sighs.

An umbrella forgotten, it twirls in the dark,
And a rubber band dares to make a remark.
Lost odds and ends, in a jumble ensure,
Each piece a riddle we try to demure.

Forgotten dreams hop, like frogs on a log,
Mooning at shadows, they dance through the fog.
Witty retorts slip through dust-coated seams,
Where humor is hidden in wild, waking dreams.

A duet of echoes sings sweetly along,
To the rhythm of whispers, a jolly old song.
In this cacophony, a lightness prevails,
Finding the funny in forgotten tales.

Apertures of Abandoned Poetry.

In corners where the old books frown,
There's laughter from the words upside down.
Forgotten rhymes tickle the air,
They giggle like they just don't care.

The pencils are plotting a silly scheme,
To reinvent the lost poet's dream.
Papers dance with a quirky flip,
On the edge of a rainbow slip.

Ink stains whisper in a merry tone,
"Who knew sheets could feel so alone?"
Yet their tales of yore just beg for play,
As they prance in their own dusty ballet.

With quills that quack and letters that sing,
An orchestra of nonsense they bring.
In this attic of quirky delight,
Words play hide-and-seek every night.

Whispers in Dusty Shelves

Upon the shelves where cobwebs bloom,
A rumor of rhymes begins to zoom.
Old sonnets in slippers, a jaunty start,
Chasing the cat, jumping apart.

Each dust bunny breathes a secret sigh,
Of limericks lost that learned to fly,
While the grammar gremlins throw wordy glee,
In a raucous party, just wait and see!

A prose parade marches on the floor,
"Have we been here before? Let's explore!"
Laughing letters slide with style,
While mischief winks with a cheeky smile.

Narratives prance without a care,
Whispering tales that tickle the air.
Join the tomes in their laughter parade,
For there's fun in every line that's made.

Echoes from the Shelves of Silence

Echoes hum where the quiet reigns,
Words bounce back with comical pains.
"Why so serious?" the verbs do tease,
As they pirouette with humorous ease.

The metaphors chuckle, dressed in a suit,
As adjectives play tag, fast on their feet.
"Let's swap our meanings and create a jest!"
The laughter of language is truly the best.

In the stillness, a giggle breaks free,
A pun from a noun reclining with glee.
Riddles roll like marbles, so perfectly round,
Creating chaos in the silence profound.

Syllables stumble, take a wild fall,
Piling up words for a side-splitting brawl.
With echoes that bounce like a ball of yarn,
In this whimsical place, there's never a barn!

Lost Letters in the Shadows

In shadows where the lost letters creep,
They gather for secrets instead of sleep.
"Let's spell a word that makes folks smile!"
A silly little game, it's worth the while.

Each envelope hides a joke or two,
While scribbles plot a mischief to pursue.
"Dear Recipient, let's make a mess,
Words of absurdity are nothing less!"

A note slips out with a wink and a nudge,
"Can we get more giggles? Let's not budge!"
Stanzas dance in a lively refrain,
Creating a ruckus like a runaway train.

In the dusk where creativity roams,
Each letter finds its way back home.
To find joy in the lost, come join the fun,
With laughter aplenty, we've only begun!

Palimpsest of Forgotten Stories

In dusty corners, tales reside,
Old shoes left behind, nowhere to hide.
A cat naps soundly on ancient lore,
While socks plot mischief, they can't ignore.

Forgotten fables, slightly askew,
The toaster's tale of burnt bread, it's true.
The clock ticks loudly, forgetting its time,
It hums a tune in a rhythmless rhyme.

A hairball rolls, it laughs at the past,
Whispers of secrets that just couldn't last.
A lamp flickers, a jest in the night,
Kindling dreams of the curious light.

So here we dwell in whimsical thought,
Whims tumbling over, joyfully caught.
Unraveled yarns, like a kite in the sky,
Chasing the wind, oh, how they fly!

Treasuries of Secure Silence

Beneath the floorboards, treasures abound,
A horde of silence, without a sound.
Buttons and marbles, a curious stash,
Misplacing our worries in a colorful crash.

Crumbs of old cookies, laughter they bring,
The ghosts of sweet snacks merrily swing.
A map made of crumbs, leading to fun,
Explorations await, a quest has begun.

In shadows and corners, giggles reside,
As dust motes dance, the sun's glowing guide.
A note on the wall, scribbled with glee,
'Find more lost laughter, we'll share a cup of tea!'

Old chairs creak softly, a tune so light,
Joining the giggles that linger in flight.
Here joy is a treasure, securely enclosed,
In boxes of whispers that chuckle and doze.

Testament of Tangible Thoughts

Notes written sideways in ink that's run,
Lay scattered like puzzles meant for some fun.
A shoe-shaped memo says 'work like a pro',
While bell socks chirp, 'you don't run too slow!'

A sticky note war cries, 'Go make some cake!'
While the spoon draws plans for a big, wild shake.
Ideas tumble out, wearing funny hats,
Dance with the papers, a party of cats!

A journal filled with doodles and dreams,
Bizarre little moments that burst at the seams.
Flip through the pages, they wiggle and grin,
Inviting you to let the laughter in.

A dog-eared letter that hums a soft tune,
Underneath it all, a big smiling moon.
So here we scribble, where chaos can reign,
In a realm where giggles wash away the pain.

Echoing Bones of the Narrative

Walls whisper secrets, tales they can't take,
Old movie posters begin to awake.
A skeleton dances in mismatched shoes,
Quipping and quarreling, singing the blues.

Chairs recall gossip that traveled like jet,
With grumpy old cushions, a laughter duet.
A broom with a twist, in the corner it waits,
For dust bunnies' parties, with all of their mates.

A statue of a cat, with a grin so wide,
Hiding its secrets, with nowhere to hide.
Chasing lost echoes of misfit desires,
While batteries chuckle, outlasting their fires.

Here in the silence, each bump and each thud,
Builds a mosaic of joy from the mud.
So join in the fun, let the joy keep you whole,
For hidden in quirks is the heart of our soul!

Unraveled Threads of Thought

In a box of thoughts all tangled tight,
A sock and a cat both start a fight.
Old dreams giggle in corners unseen,
Like notes from a band that never has been.

Forgotten jokes hide behind the door,
Whispering riddles from days of yore.
A rubber chicken, a broken clock,
Remind me of times I just couldn't rock.

Each scribbled line brings a smile or two,
A diary entry from a frog's point of view.
With a wink and a nudge, the past comes alive,
In this jumble of words where memories thrive.

So let's dance with the chaos, the silly, the mad,
Embrace the absurd; it's not really sad.
For laughter is waiting in these dusty stacks,
With a tickle of joy from the old genies' cracks.

Tattered Pages of Longing

Old books with covers that droop and sigh,
Whisper sweet secrets, oh my, oh my!
Penguin in pajamas and elephants bold,
Tell tales of treasure and gnomes turned old.

Pages crinkle like grandma's old smile,
With stories of hiccups and trips down the aisle.
Lovers once pure now longing for snacks,
Like puddles of chocolate in paper-crash wracks.

From quests for the keys to unlock the snacks,
To poems 'bout gerbils in shoe-shaped backpacks.
Every turn of a page brings giggles anew,
As I ponder deep secrets—like where'd my sock go too?

The ink is all smudged, but the laughter is clear,
These riddles of longing bring joy, my dear.
So curl up with nonsense from long lost times,
Where whimsy and wit play in mismatched rhymes.

The Archive of Lost Echoes

Sounds of old echoes bounce off the walls,
Like the giggling voices who've forgotten their calls.
A snort from the past dances in playful spree,
While a whispering ghost is just over there—see?

Each chuckle and snicker hangs thick in the air,
Where secrets are giggling without any care.
A joke that fell flat now floats with great glee,
Tickling the edges of all memory.

In corners of silence where mischief once crept,
Lies a joke book that's actually wept.
With each giggle nutty, each pun a delight,
These echoes of laughter run wild in the night.

So listen real close, let the past bring a cheer,
For echoes of laughter still linger near.
A chorus of whimsy, a symphony grand,
Turns moments to merriment with a wave of a hand.

Secrets in the Beams

Up in the rafters where dust bunnies play,
Secrets are swirling and laughing away.
A pickle jar full of unsent postcards,
Dreaming of journeys, yet stuck in the yard.

The beams hold the tales of cats on the prowl,
Of owls who once hooted and let out a howl.
Each creak of the floor tells a story or two,
In the attic of giggles, where whimsy comes through.

Mismatched socks trying to frolic in style,
A broom making mischief, a Goose on the dial.
So many shenanigans float in the air,
These secrets in beams giggle—if you dare.

Let's unearth the chuckles, the quirks lodged in time,
In this attic of fun, where we find every rhyme.
So lift up your spirits, don the fable's crown,
As we dance with these secrets in our sleepy town.

Shadows of Unspoken Stories

Amidst the dust and grins, they play,
Old phrases dance in a silly ballet.
Missing nouns and verbs in a swirl,
Whispers of laughter in a jumbled whirl.

Cushions with cat tales, never to tell,
A rolling pin's secret, oh what the hell!
Waltzing socks and mismatched shoes,
Words forget their partners, they just snooze.

In the corners, a pun waits to crop,
While jokes on jumbled paper flop.
Catchy phrases, with giggles they tease,
In this wooden palace, they dance with ease.

With each cobweb, a punchline lurks,
Silly ones hide where the old chair jerks.
Unseen chortles bounce off the walls,
Where stories wait, and giggling calls.

Fragments of Oblivion

Snippets of banter lost in the air,
Lacking a punchline, but still they dare.
A pickle jar full of silly delight,
Where laughter and whimsy take flight.

Forgotten tales in a cardboard box,
A coat with secrets, an old pair of socks.
Word fragments waltz with quirks quite absurd,
Each corner echoes a long-lost word.

Socks munch on riddles, oh what a sight,
Comical mishaps bring pure delight.
Under a loose floorboard, jokes try to hide,
Tickling the dustbunnies, laughing with pride.

Echoes of silliness spring from the gloom,
As misplaced sentences find their room.
A yawn turns to chuckle, quite unforeseen,
In the land of the lost, where fun reigns supreme.

Voices Beneath the Rafters

Chirpy conversations in a creaky chair,
Muffled giggles linger in the air.
Tales from the rafters, riddles galore,
Whispers of humor, they ask for more.

Sassy shadows slide with each jest,
Unruly phrases put to the test.
An echo of laughter, tucked away neat,
Where goofy gnomes tap their tiny feet.

A tattered hat holds a curious lore,
With jokes that tumble, their sides they tore.
Mice debate puns in a grand pas de deux,
In the heights where the unseen winds blew.

Some words may giggle and skip to the beat,
Creating a symphony of humorous feats.
Beneath the rafters, where air heads collide,
Voices of laughter, our silly guide.

Treasures Beneath the Eaves

Old hats with a twinkle, a wink, and a grin,
Jokes land in corners where silliness begins.
Forgotten treasures, they sparkle and shine,
In the nook of the eaves, they intertwine.

A rubber chicken makes quite the scene,
Crafting a ruckus where dust bunnies glean.
Each giggle reveals a forgotten delight,
In places all strange, where shadows take flight.

Marbles of mischief roll left and right,
Dialogue stumbles, but laughter takes flight.
Puns play peek-a-boo; oh what a jest,
Among quirky fragments they feel quite blessed.

Light hearted laughter drifts through the beams,
In this whimsical world, where fun reigns supreme.
All hidden treasures, just waiting to tease,
Under the eaves, they chuckle with ease.

Riddles of the Hidden Nook

In corners where old socks conspire,
Lurking tales of a lost desire.
Dust bunnies dance with a playful sass,
Whispering secrets of the glass.

A shoe without its partner waits,
With tales of dates and silly fates.
Worn out hats with feathers ask,
Why do humans wear such a mask?

Imaginary friends line the walls,
They throw parties when nightfall calls.
An echo of laughter fills the air,
While forgotten dreams have more flair.

Cracks in the ceiling hold witty jokes,
Telling tales of sly old folks.
With each creak of the wooden floor,
The house has lived a life full of lore.

Fleeting Thoughts in the Gloom

In shadows where giggles linger near,
A dusty globe spins tales we hold dear.
Mismatched buttons have stories to weave,
Of clothes that no one dares to believe.

Dreams of monsters peek from the dark,
While old toys share tales with a spark.
A couch sings ballads of slumbering past,
Where time was slow, but fun was vast.

An umbrella hides a rain of sweet cries,
Beneath it, a world where silliness flies.
Jars of marbles roll with a clatter,
Perhaps they're more than just idle chatter.

In corners where memories nearly fade,
Each whisper a game, each giggle a parade.
With candles flickering bright on the shelf,
Strange riddles of life echo themselves.

Memoirs of a Silent Room

Within these four walls, silence pranks,
Dusty chairs hold hilarious flanks.
A lonely shoe giggles, half a pair,
What mischief did you see out there?

Lampshades wobble, whispering gossip,
While quirky clocks tick-tock with a skip.
A picture's frown turns into a grin,
Wondering who'll come in next for a spin.

In corners stuffed with faded cheer,
Old novels sigh as they bring near.
A curtain rustles like a sly tease,
Could it be waiting to hear a sneeze?

Remember when the sofa was a ship?
Explorers laughing, on wild trips.
This room may stay quiet, but don't you fret,
It's packed with moments we won't forget.

Echoes of Unspoken Dreams

Where fantasies tumble beneath the floor,
A giggle erupts from the old wardrobe's door.
Rumbles of laughter, a backdrop of quirks,
In this whimsical world, nobody lurks.

Socks chase each other in playful bounds,
As pillows plot on cozy grounds.
A sleepy cat dreams of chasing the moon,
While dust moats whirl to a silent tune.

Back in the corner, an old calculator hums,
Reciting the jokes of far-off sums.
While scraps of paper waltz with delight,
Filling the silence with tales of the night.

In shadows where mutterings softly play,
They juggle around in a silly ballet.
Each echo a chuckle, a giggle of light,
In the realms of the forgotten, all feels just right.

The Language of Forgotten Ink

Old pens gather dust, oh what a sight,
They once wrote tales, now they just bite.
A quill with a wink, a fountain that drips,
Whispers of laughter from every scribbled script.

Inkblots like shadows, dancing around,
Conversations missed, without a sound.
They tell of a waltz, or maybe a brawl,
But the paper's too shy to share it all.

Crayons chuckle from a box in the back,
Their colors now faded, they've lost their knack.
In this quirky corner where chaos reigns,
Each scribble a secret, in whimsical chains.

A dictionary grins, with a pun or two,
Defining the joy in the silly things you do.
Forgotten ink sings, with a burble and squawk,
As it dances along with the ticks of the clock.

Shadows of Untold Stories

Underneath layers, where secrets creep,
Tales in the shadows silently weep.
Characters hiding with quirky grins,
Plot twists forgotten like lost little twins.

The bookshelf giggles as pages unwind,
A book's spine creaks, it's been one of a kind.
Words tumble out like confetti in flight,
Spilling old jokes they can't quite recite.

Stories that skipped, like stones on the lake,
Leave trails of laughter, oh what a mistake!
The chair in the corner seems slightly bemused,
It once had a guest, now it feels used.

And every old letter, with a crease or two,
Offers a riddle, or maybe a clue.
The shadows chuckle, with tales left unheard,
In a world full of whispers, each word is absurd.

Parables in Attic Dust

In the dusty corners, where relics nest,
Lies a moral or two, if you'd dare to invest.
A shoebox of bliss, with snapshots of fun,
Each image a giggle, a race never run.

Dust bunnies ponder, with wisdom so sly,
They say, 'Never trust when the toaster goes dry.'
A forgotten sock winks, a hero it seems,
From adventurous travels in wild, funny dreams.

A mirror reflects both the past and the now,
It laughs at the styles; oh my, how they wow!
Each crack in its surface holds a tale to unfold,
Of fashion disasters and laughter retold.

When dust motes are dancing, just pause for a while,
They're swirling through stories with dust-bunny style.
The parables linger, in whispers they trust,
With echoes of humor, adorned in fine dust.

Echoes of Abandoned Verses

In the silence of corners, words long forgot,
Echo with laughter, a jolly whole lot.
Verses abandoned, yet never alone,
Compose a symphony where shadows are grown.

A limerick chuckles, sat lightly on shelves,
While syntax and rhyme are just talking to selves.
Adjectives wiggle, while nouns start to sway,
In the absence of writing, they still love to play.

Old stories shiver, in lines left to chill,
With puns that are timeless, they dance at will.
The old typewriter sighs, it's gathering rust,
But deep down inside, it's all still a must.

Each echo reflected, in memory's haze,
Crafts a new journey in ridiculous ways.
Abandoned ideas, like treasures now lost,
Are waiting for laughter, no matter the cost.

Timeless Murmurs of the Past

In a box filled with dust and glee,
Caught whispers of language, lost at sea.
Old phrases dance, a silly waltz,
While grammar cringes, blame it on impulse.

A rubber chicken named 'Mirth' slides by,
With punny memories that make us sigh.
Goofy notes penned with a crooked pen,
Invite us to laugh at our past again.

Letters leap with joy, then plop,
Like soda pop left out, they flop.
Each quip and jest a treasure chest,
Tickling our hearts, it's simply the best.

So we giggle at rhymes both comical and bright,
As echoes of humor take playful flight.
Hidden gems from an old dusty shelf,
Laughter uncovered, back to ourselves.

The Chamber of Forgotten Sentiments

In a corner where feelings went to hide,
Rusty coins jingle with forgotten pride.
Love notes with doodles, now too obscure,
Flashing winks from a time unsure.

Here lies a trophy for the silliest grin,
A snapshot of laughter beneath the skin.
Warm hugs wrapped in ribbons of time,
Slightly crooked but oh so sublime.

Socks with holes tell tales of surprise,
And once-beloved jokes wear silly ties.
A dance party winks from a dusty book,
Inviting us all to take a goofy look.

These echoes of whimsy, so light and dear,
Bring back the laughter we once held near.
In this chamber of smiles, let's play with glee,
Where nostalgia's a prankster, wild and free.

The Relics of Rhyme and Reason

Forgotten verses lie in a heap,
Quirky couplets that never sleep.
Worn out phrases, like tired clowns,
Still try to juggle their silly frowns.

A sonnet about spaghetti spills cheer,
And limericks teasing their thin veneer.
Stale jokes tumble like socks from drawers,
Tickling the fancies they first had in scores.

Words once whispered in corners of glee,
Now tumble out like they're trying to flee.
Each line a giggle, a snicker, a cheer,
Remnants of rhyme that bring us near.

With each swirl of dust, new laughter is born,
As we sift through the relics, somewhat worn.
No need to reason, let the fun commence,
For laughter is timeless, it makes perfect sense.

Smudged Inscriptions on Old Wood

Beneath the grime, where laughter once lived,
Inscribed on planks, old jokes are retrieved.
Witty carvings, though faded and gray,
Still spoon feed chuckles, come what may.

Scribbled reminders of silly debates,
Like why the chicken crossed—who cares? It waits!
Each knot in the wood, a giggle set free,
Tales of a time that once tickled me.

Graffiti of mirth, a scribbler's delight,
Where sunsets dance and the stars come bright.
Ticklish sentiments on the hearth's old floor,
Whispering rhymes just like a folklore.

As we dust off the silliness long left behind,
Let's celebrate gaffes that perfectly bind.
The smudged old inscriptions call out our name,
With laughter as fuel, we'll play this grand game!

Dusty Chronicles of Yesterday

In a box where time forgot,
A sock entwined with a plot.
Whispers of rhymes, a funny mix,
Old jokes and puns with old broomsticks.

Crumbs of laugh in the corners hide,
Each tale now takes a spinny ride.
Like a cat with an itch, they dance and twirl,
Laughter erupts in an old, dusty swirl.

Riddles wrapped in mothball dust,
Finding meaning was a must.
Each line left giggling, a teasing flirt,
As trinkets giggle in their old shirt.

Forgotten tales in a tattered book,
In shadows of shelves, a sneaky look.
Pages flipping, with a giggling sound,
Yesterday's whispers still bounce around.

The Language of Shadows

Underneath the cobweb's sway,
A ghostly cat starts to play.
Whispers bounce from wall to wall,
Echoes of laughter, a joyful call.

Ink pot spills secrets, plain as day,
As shadows wiggle and sway.
A clown's nose rolls, what a sight!
In a world where wrong feels right.

Giggling words from a crumpled scroll,
Each quip and quirk, a jester's role.
With a flourish, a pun takes flight,
In the luminescence of the moonlight.

Old shoes tap a rhythm strange,
While dust bunnies perform their range.
In this language of quirky fun,
Every forgotten word leaves one undone.

Hidden Verses of Time

In a nook where laughter hides,
Old quirks on an adventurous ride.
A rhyme slips from behind a shoe,
Nudging memories, both old and new.

Tick-tock, the clock begins to dash,
While spoons argue in a busy clash.
A noodle notes a symphony,
As words twist, uncoiling glee.

Potato jokes and silly puns,
Wrapped in warmth like the sun.
Each line brings giggles, a joyous spree,
In this chamber, wild and free.

Sprinkled dust, a surprise or two,
Forgetfulness, oh what a view.
Dancing words through years unkind,
In each forgotten nook, they unwind.

Cadence of the Unremembered

In corners, they hide, these quirky words,
Spinning tales like fluttering birds.
Each chuckle wrapped in the silence deep,
A plucky remark that refuses to sleep.

The ceiling's cracks hold stories bold,
Of shenanigans that won't grow old.
Jigsaws, misfits, and silly dreams,
All humming along with mismatched themes.

In a hat, a rabbit runs wild,
Tickling thoughts, a humor child.
With giggles tripping over their toes,
Each line smiles, each tale grows.

Forgotten rhymes in a playful chase,
Bringing warmth and a gentle grace.
In the garden of memory where smiles roam,
Each unremembered word finds a home.

Memory's Cloistered Corners

In corners where the dust bunnies play,
Lie secrets from a yesterday.
Old shoes with stories, lonely and lost,
Chasing memories, whatever the cost.

A sock that vanished in a great fight,
Hiding from laundry, what a silly sight!
A moth-eaten hat with a whimsical flair,
Claims it was worn by the prince of despair.

Ghosts of the past in a jumbled pile,
Each one of them wearing a very strange smile.
A note in crayon that simply says 'Yo!',
From the days when I believed I could grow.

So here in this nook of delightful disgrace,
I sift through the remnants, a wild goose chase.
Finding laughter where shadows once sat,
In corners where words play, how 'bout that!

Forgotten Sounds of Solitude

Whispers of laughter trapped in the air,
Echoes of shoes that no longer are there.
A squeaky floorboard, a ghost with a grin,
Tells tales of chaos where silence has been.

A chuckle that jingles from a tin can top,
Fizzles and bubbles, it never will stop.
The creak of a chair that rocks all alone,
Wonders if it once had a friend of its own.

A ball of yarn that just won't keep still,
Rolls into corners, oh what a thrill!
Tickles of memories skip along walls,
As I dance with the shadows that stumble and fall.

Lost in the rhythm of a joke long expired,
Each laugh is a spark, a moment admired.
In the silence, there's music we can't quite recall,
In the sounds of solitude, we hear it all.

The Gallery of Ghosted Thoughts

On walls of white, ideas paint a scene,
Like poltergeist portraits, all caught in between.
A thought in a frame that forgot its own name,
Flutters like stickers, all wild and untame.

A daydream that's dressed in mismatched socks,
Wanders the gallery in flip-flop talks.
With laughter that echoes from a frame of a cat,
Who schemes and dreams of a world made of rat.

Arrows of humor fly high on the wall,
Where giggles and guffaws mingle and sprawl.
Each canvas a tale of the crazy and bold,
An exhibit of nonsense, all laughter retold.

So come take a stroll through this whimsical space,
Where thoughts with a giggle dance all over the place.
In the gallery's light, the memories gleam,
Good humor lives on, it's more than a dream!

Dusty Recollections

In a box marked 'memories,' I found some old toys,
Rusty and dusty, but oh, what a noise!
A squeaky bear that croaks out a tune,
Sings silly songs beneath a bright moon.

Old letters forgotten, with ink barely bold,
Whisper their secrets, all stories retold.
A crumpled-up paper that claims it's a prize,
For the best pizza maker that could make pies size-wise.

Recipe cards faded, with spills on the sides,
Chart how to conquer the world with great fries.
Tattered and torn, but they still hold a laugh,
Each bite a reminder of our funny path.

So here in this dust, I unearth and I cheer,
For all of the memories that brought us good cheer.
With humor preserved in the depths of the grime,
I toast to the past, one laugh at a time!

www.ingramcontent.com/pod-product-compliance
Lightning Source LLC
Chambersburg PA
CBHW070312120526
44590CB00017B/2647